A CHILD'S DAY
IN A SOUTH AFRICAN CITY

To my sons, Samuel and Joseph, and all the children of South Africa

Benchmark Books
Marshall Cavendish
99 White Plains Road
Tarrytown, New York 10591
www.marshallcavendish.com

Library of Congress Cataloging-in-Publication Data

Wulfsohn, Gisèle.
In a South African city / by Gisèle Wulfsohn.
p. cm. — (A child's day)
Includes index.
Summary: Presents a day in the life of a child living in Johannesburg, discussing
the social life, customs, religion, history, and language of South Africa.
ISBN 0-7614-1407-X
1. South Africa—Social life and customs—Juvenile literature.
[1. South Africa—Social life and customs.] I. Title. II. Series.

DT1752 .W85 2002   968—dc21   2001043943

Designed by Sophie Pelham

Printed in Singapore

1 3 5 7 9 8 6 4 2

AUTHOR ACKNOWLEDGMENTS
I would like to thank Bongani Mofokeng, and his aunt, uncle, and cousins—Manana, David, Flory, and Thabi Coplan—
for allowing me a glimpse of their lives. To David Coplan, special thanks for all your time, advice, and input.
To Mrs. Ailsa Steyn (principal of Emmarentia Primary School), Miss Layla van der Merwe (Bongani's teacher), and
Bongani's classmates—thank you for your cooperation.
To my husband, Mark Turpin, thank you for your ever-present love and support.

A CHILD'S DAY
IN A SOUTH AFRICAN CITY

Gisèle Wulfsohn

BENCHMARK BOOKS

MARSHALL CAVENDISH
NEW YORK

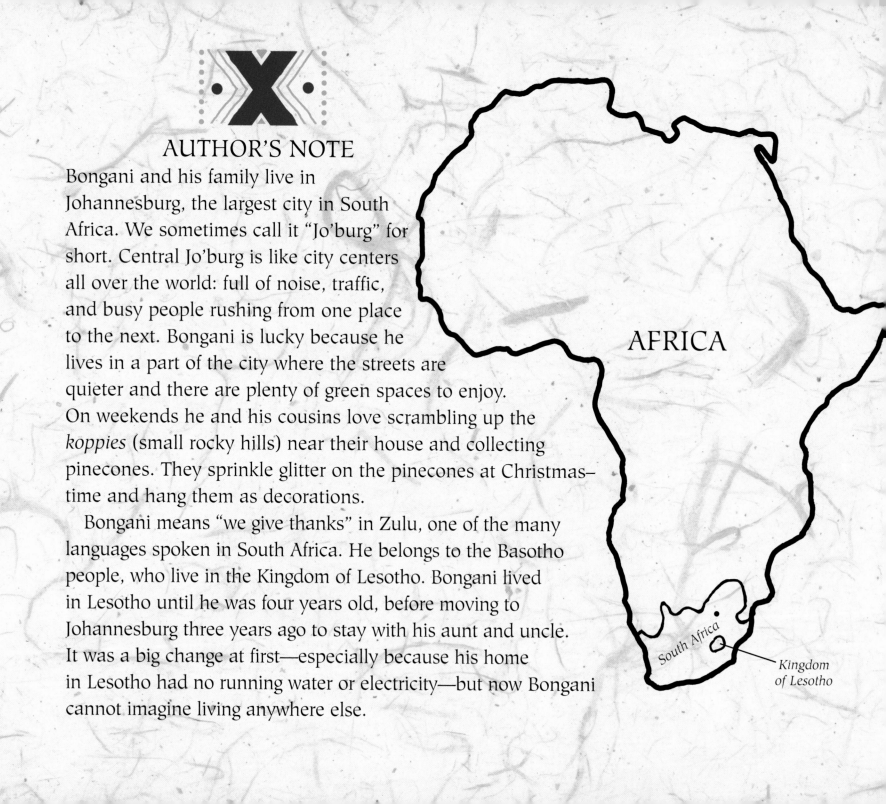

AUTHOR'S NOTE

Bongani and his family live in
Johannesburg, the largest city in South
Africa. We sometimes call it "Jo'burg" for
short. Central Jo'burg is like city centers
all over the world: full of noise, traffic,
and busy people rushing from one place
to the next. Bongani is lucky because he
lives in a part of the city where the streets are
quieter and there are plenty of green spaces to enjoy.
On weekends he and his cousins love scrambling up the
koppies (small rocky hills) near their house and collecting
pinecones. They sprinkle glitter on the pinecones at Christmas–
time and hang them as decorations.

   Bongani means "we give thanks" in Zulu, one of the many
languages spoken in South Africa. He belongs to the Basotho
people, who live in the Kingdom of Lesotho. Bongani lived
in Lesotho until he was four years old, before moving to
Johannesburg three years ago to stay with his aunt and uncle.
It was a big change at first—especially because his home
in Lesotho had no running water or electricity—but now Bongani
cannot imagine living anywhere else.

AFRICA

South Africa

Kingdom
of Lesotho

Bongani Mofokeng is seven years old.

He lives in a quiet part of Johannesburg called Westdene with his uncle David, his aunt Manana, and his two cousins Thabi, age ten, and Flory, age seventeen. David is a professor at the University of the *Witwatersrand*. Manana runs a food van for minibus taxi drivers in the city.

THE WITWATERSRAND is a big, rocky ridge which surrounds Johannesburg. It contains some of the richest gold deposits in the world.

Bongani and Thabi are both fast asleep in their bunk beds when
Difedile, the family's housekeeper, comes to wake them up
at six o'clock. After a yawn and a stretch, they get dressed and go
to the bathroom to wash their faces and brush their teeth.

When they are washed and dressed, Bongani and Thabi are ready for breakfast. Bongani eats his cereal quickly so that he can watch cartoons on television before he has to leave for school.

Bongani prefers cereal, but many more South Africans start their day with mielie meal porridge. Mielie means "corn" in Afrikaans (one of the languages spoken in South Africa), and is one of South Africa's biggest crops.

Bongani and Thabi attend Emmarentia Elementary School about two miles away. While waiting for Uncle David to drive them, they climb into the back of the *bakkie* (truck) to enjoy the morning air.

When Uncle David is ready, Bongani and Thabi get into the cab of the truck and head to school.

When the school bell rings, all the children organize themselves into lines in the courtyard. Each child has a special place in the line, which means that there is no need for anyone to run or push. Once there is silence, they recite the school prayer. The prayer was specially written so that it has meaning for everyone, no matter what religion they practice.

The first lesson of the day is English. Bongani's teacher, Miss *van der Merwe*, tells the class that they will be studying the letter c. To start them thinking, she gathers everyone together on the carpet and reads them a funny story about a character named Clever Cat.

VAN DER MERWE is a common last name among the Afrikaner people of South Africa. All the van der Merwes are descended from the same man, Willem van der Merwe, who came from Holland to settle in South Africa over three hundred years ago. These settlers from Holland and other countries in Europe developed a language called Afrikaans and became known as the Afrikaners.

When the story is over, the children go back to their desks and write down all the other words they can think of that begin with c. Bongani raises his hand to ask whether he can do some drawings too.

After English they put away their books and put on their art aprons. Miss van der Merwe shows them how to draw a clown face on a paper plate.

11

During recess, Bongani rushes outside to the climbing ropes to play *Shaka Zulu* with his friends.

SHAKA ZULU King Shaka was a powerful chief who once ruled over the Zulu people—one of the main groups of people in South Africa. Bongani's game is based on a recent television series about the adventures of King Shaka and his Zulu warriors. When they reach the top of the tire tunnel, they jump off and yell, "Bayete Nkosi," which means "Hail the chief!" in Zulu.

Back inside after recess, it is time for Bongani's favorite subject: computer skills. This morning the class is trying out a new math program.

The next lesson is PE (physical education). Bongani concentrates hard on every step as he walks across the balancing beam because he does not want to fall off!

In the final half hour Miss van der Merwe reads the class a story from a book called *Water Adventures*. Water is their special project this term, so the children learn something new about water every day.

At one o'clock the bell rings for the end of school, and the students pack their bags.

After school Uncle David takes Bongani to see Manana at her food van. Sometimes Bongani helps Manana sweep the pavement around the van, but today his friend James has asked him to help wash Manana's car. It is James's job to wash the minibus taxis while the drivers are having their lunch.

16

Today Manana has prepared her specialty, the *African Plate*. She and Bongani sit down together to enjoy their food while Manana's assistant watches over the big cooking pots on the stove.

AFRICAN PLATE Manana's African Plate is made up of meat stew, mielie pap (a stiff, white porridge made from corn), mashed potatoes, beets, and chakalaka, a delicious dish made from tomatoes, onions, and chilies.

After lunch Uncle David and Bongani pick up Thabi from school and head for home. They stop off at the supermarket on their way to buy some groceries. In the candy section they choose some chocolate for Manana as a present—and a bar for each of them too!

Kirsty, the family's pet rabbit, is hungry by the time they arrive back home. Bongani gives her some cauliflower and cabbage to eat.

Then he crosses the street to his friend Lucky Boy's house. Lucky is very happy to see Bongani because he has new sunglasses and wants to show them off.

When the day starts to cool down, Bongani and Thabi take their new puppy, Spencer, for a walk up Banbury Street. As they walk past the high walls in front of the houses, Spencer wags his tail because he can hear the neighborhood dogs (*dintja*) barking.

Security is important in Johannesburg. Many people protect their houses with high walls, gates, or electric fences.

At about six o'clock Bongani settles down to do his English homework. He wants to finish it before Manana comes home so that she can check it and sign it.

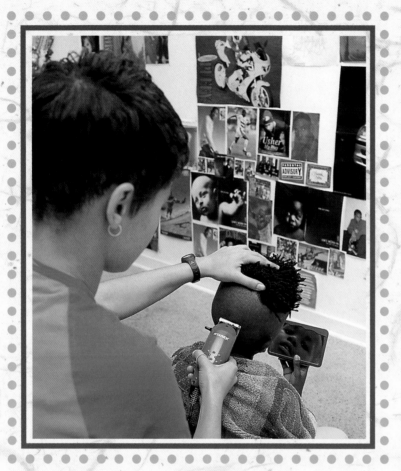

Every couple of weeks Flory shaves Bongani's head with an electric razor, rubs Vaseline into the bare skin, and then puts hair wax on his dreadlocks (thick, braided strands of hair) to keep them shiny.

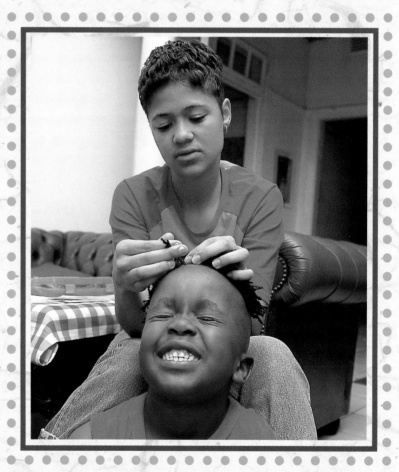

Bongani has the same hairstyle as Lucas Radebe, the captain of *Bafana Bafana*: shaved around the sides with a mop of dreadlocks on top.

BAFANA BAFANA means "boys boys" in Zulu and is the nickname of the South African national soccer team.

David has made spaghetti for dinner and everyone sits down together.
They are all so busy during the week that it is often easier for the children
to eat earlier by themselves.

After dinner Bongani, Flory, Thabi, and baby cousin Nikita, who is visiting, dance the *kwasa kwasa* and watch some *kwaito* videos.

KWASA KWASA is a style of music and dance from central Africa. You shuffle backward and forward while swaying your shoulders and hips to the rhythms of the music.

KWAITO is a style of black South African dance music that is very popular with young people. The music is created in a studio using synthesizers and computers. The words are usually sung in Tsotsitaal, a South African street slang.

Bongani could dance all night, but Manana reminds him that he needs to take a bath.

Afterward he treats Manana to a foot massage. He teases her by saying that he expects payment, but really he enjoys spoiling his *rakhadi* (aunt) after her exhausting day.

25

There is just enough time for a quick family music session before bed. Bongani plays the *balafon*, Uncle David has chosen the *apentemma*, Thabi strums a guitar, and Manana tries out a *dondon*.

BALAFON A wooden percussion instrument that is similar to a xylophone.
APENTEMMA A traditional drum from Ghana in West Africa.
DONDON A Nigerian "talking" drum, which has tones that can sound like a person's voice.

At nine o'clock Bongani
and Thabi kiss everyone good
night and go to bed. Thabi
reads to Bongani until he
falls asleep.

Robala hantle Bongani.
(Good night, Bongani.)

MORE ABOUT SOUTH AFRICA

SOUTH AFRICA, THE LAND

The country of South Africa lies at the southern tip of the continent of Africa. It has many different kinds of landscape: a long and sunny coastline; vast mountain ranges; regions of lush farmland as well as large flat areas of scrub; national parklands, where herds of wild animals like elephants and buffalo roam; and a huge desert (the Karoo). It is also rich in natural resources, including gold, diamonds, and almost every useful type of mineral.

SOUTH AFRICA, THE PAST

In the very beginning, the land of South Africa was inhabited by black tribespeople. The first white people to settle in the country came from Holland, France, Belgium, and Germany in 1652. These settlers, who became known as the Afrikaners (or Boers), began farming the land, and fought brutal wars with the black tribespeople who already lived and worked on it. When the British settled in South Africa about two hundred years later, they also wanted the land for themselves. Many more wars followed, including the Zulu Wars between the British and the Zulus (the biggest group of black people in South Africa) and the Boer Wars between the British and the Dutch settlers.

For a long time in South Africa's history, the white people ruling the country believed that they had more right than the black people to all the good things South Africa had to offer. The white government passed laws that said black South Africans had to live in different areas from white South Africans and go to separate schools. When the people protested that these laws were unfair, the government punished them severely. This system was called apartheid.

The rest of the world condemned South Africa for its apartheid laws, but the South African government ignored them. They sent many black leaders, like Nelson Mandela, to prison, and they took many black South Africans from their homes and moved them to homelands (areas miles from the cities, where the land was poor). Eventually, however, the South African people and the rest of the world protested so much that the South African government had to give in. In 1990 Nelson Mandela was set free after twenty-seven years in prison and became the first black president of South Africa. The day he became president, April 27,1994, is known as Freedom Day, and is celebrated every year.

PEOPLE IN SOUTH AFRICA

South Africa is often called the "rainbow nation" because the people who live there come from so many different races and cultures. Unfortunately, because of its troubled history, South Africa is also a land of great inequality. While some South Africans are wealthy, many are still very poor. Diseases like AIDS and tuberculosis are widespread, and many people have to manage without decent housing, clean water, or electricity.

RELIGION IN SOUTH AFRICA

Most South Africans are Christians. The churches and their leaders, such as Archbishop Desmond Tutu, gave important support to the South African people as they struggled under the apartheid system. There are also large numbers of Hindus, Muslims, Jews, and African traditionalists. Traditionalists worship their ancestors—although they are no longer alive, they remain important members of the family.

LANGUAGE IN SOUTH AFRICA

South Africa has eleven official languages. The most widely spoken are English, Afrikaans, IsiZulu, IsiXhosa, and Sesotho. (Although IsiZulu and IsiXhosa are the correct terms, people usually refer to these languages as Zulu and Xhosa.) Bongani speaks fluent Sesotho as well as English.

ENGLISH is spoken by almost half of the white people living in South Africa (the others speak Afrikaans). Many more South Africans know how to speak English, but it is not the language they speak at home.

AFRIKAANS is spoken mainly by the Afrikaner people. It developed as a mixture of the languages spoken by the first European settlers: Dutch, French, German, and English.

IsiZULU is spoken by the Zulu people. The Zulus live mainly in the KwaZulu Natal Province in the east of the country, where the Zulu royal family has its palace.

IsiXHOSA is spoken by the Xhosa people who live in the southern area of South Africa. IsiXhosa is difficult to speak for non-Xhosa people because it has so many click sounds.

SESOTHO is the language of the Basotho people who live in the Kingdom of Lesotho (the small country within South Africa where Bongani was born). It is also spoken widely in South Africa.

SOME SESOTHO WORDS AND PHRASES
Dumela. Lebitso la ka ke Bongani.
   —Hello. My name is Bongani.
O phela jwang?—How are you?
Ke phela hantle.—I am fine.
Ke leboha haholo.
   —Thank you very much.

GLOSSARY

African Plate–Manana's specialty dish, made up of popular African foods like meat stew and mielie pap

Afrikaans–a language spoken in South Africa

Afrikaners–the white African people whose ancestors came to South Africa from Holland, Belgium, France, and Germany

apartheid–an Afrikaans word meaning "being apart." It is used to describe the way the previous white South African government kept black and white South Africans apart

apentemma–a traditional drum from Ghana in West Africa

Archbishop Desmond Tutu–the Christian leader who helped fight apartheid

Bafana Bafana–the nickname of the South African national soccer team

bakkie–a truck

balafon–an African musical instrument that is similar to a xylophone

Basotho–the people who live in Lesotho

Bayete Nkosi–"Hail the Chief!" in Zulu

Boers–the Dutch farmers who settled in South Africa

chakalaka–a spicy mixture of vegetables

dintja–dogs in Sesotho

dondon–a "talking" drum from Nigeria

dreadlocks–thick, braided strands of hair

koppie–a small rocky hill

kwaito–a popular style of South African dance music

kwasa kwasa–a style of music and dance from central Africa

Lesotho–a small country within South Africa

mielie meal–ground corn

mielie pap–a stiff, white porridge made from mielie meal

Nelson Mandela–South Africa's first black president

rakhadi–aunt in Sesotho

Robala hantle–"Good night" in Sesotho

Sesotho–one of the languages spoken in South Africa and by the Basotho people of Lesotho

Shaka Zulu–a famous Zulu chief

Tsotsitaal–a South African slang language

The Witwatersrand–a rocky ridge surrounding Johannesburg that is mined for gold and minerals

Zulu–the largest group of black people in South Africa. Zulu is also the name of the language they speak

FIND OUT MORE

Dahl, Michael S. *South Africa*. Mankato, Minnesota: Capstone Press, 1998.

Holland, Gina. *Nelson Mandela*. Austin, Texas: Raintree Steck-Vaughn, 1997.

Oluonye, Mary N. *South Africa*. Minneapolis, Minnesota: Lerner, 1999.

INDEX

Afrikaner people 10, 28 30
art lesson 11

bedtime 27
breakfast 7

cartoons 7
computer lesson 13
corn 7

dancing 24
dinner 23
disease 29
dog walking 20

English lesson 10–11

food van 5, 17

geography 28
gold 5, 28

haircut 22
history of South Africa 10, 12, 28–29
homework 21

language 10, 30 31
lunch 17

meals 7, 17, 23
music 24, 26

PE lesson 14

playtime 12, 19
prayers 9

religion 9, 29

school 9–15
security 20
soccer 22
storytime 15, 27
supermarket 18

washing 6

Zulu people 12, 28, 30